The Belle Mar

Katie Bickham

The Belle Mar

PLEIADES
P R E S S

Lena-Miles Wever Todd Poetry Series

Warrensburg, Missouri & Rock Hill, South Carolina

Library of Congress Control Number:
ISBN: 978-0-8071-6049-7

Published by Pleiades Press

Department of English
University of Central Missouri
Warrensbsurg, Missouri 64093

&

Department of English
Winthrop University
Rock Hill, South Carolina 29733

Distributed by Louisiana State University Press

Cover Image: "Southern Landscape" (oil on board, 48" x 48") by
Walter Williams, 1977. Courtesy M. Hanks Gallery, Santa Monica, CA.

Book design by Sarah Nguyen
Author's photo by Bonne Fete Photography

First Pleiades Printing, 2015

Financial Assistance for this project has been provided by the Missouri
Arts Council, a state agency, and the National Endowment for the Arts.

For Keith, who is steady in bad weather. And for Alexs Pate, who gave me the keys to the house and the courage to use them.

Table of Contents

Dining Room, 1811

Even after Adellaide had washed it twice,
the stench of gunpowder held fast
to the sleeves of his fine militia jacket,
the smell filling the fanned air above the table.
Gem brought in dishes
of bisque on saucers, careful
not to let her fingers touch the food.

"I've heard they're all accounted for
from St. Charles Parish," said his father.
"And five of them your kills,"
his father said, toasting his son
with his spoon. Gem left the room
with her hands in her apron.

"Seven," said the son. "Five shot in the woods,
but two were saved and sent
for trying on the property."
"A trial?" his mother asked, dabbing broth
from her bottom lip. "For runaways?"

"Who ran away?" asked his small sister.

"The trials are a fine thing," his father said,
"so all can see. They drove the heads
of the last set onto pikes at the levee."

The son flexed his shoulders until the seams
tensed. He wished the smell
would wash out. "A fine thing," he echoed.
Gem slipped back in, refilled their water glasses.
Sweat rose in beads on the sides.

"Pike?" the little one asked.
The son held the food in his mouth,

unable to swallow until he was certain
no one would give her an answer.

Far Swamp, 1825

Only way you could find a way through
was to have something to compare everything to.
A woman knows which pains she'll survive
considering those she's known before,
knows which season's best for fruit
from swallowing it sour once or twice,
knows which man she'll stand beside
by how he stands up next to others.

Sometimes she still felt the black water rocking
the nightmare boat that brought her here.
The sailors, she recalled, knew where they stood
on the ocean 'cause of north in the stars
or on the spinning needle. True north,
she heard them say when storms blew them back.

This is the fourth death on the property in a moon cycle.
As she walks in the torch-lit crowd to carry the body
already stinking in the raw wood coffin
deep into the swamp to be buried, she knows
this is bad. This is low. Only salvation

is knowing there's badder and lower
ways to die. On the boat, when her milk sister
tried to shake captain's men, they strung
her by her thumbs, flayed her
slow with blades, flung her body in the sea.

At least this body – rotted from the day's heat
while it waited to be boxed and buried – just got beat,
fast and simple, no show to it. When they reach
the grave, dug that morning by the body's husband,
they look inside to see it half-full of gulf water.

The hole is too deep in the swamps where nothing

grows, where what stays rots and floats. They argue
for a while – "We caint put it here. – We could burn it.
– They won't like to know we burnt it."
After while, when the bugs start biting,

and to the sea rock of the husband's sad song,
they let the boxed body sink in the black
water and cover it with mud. Can't see
no stars so far in the bog, she thinks. Can't find
north now. Can't figure up how far from home

she is. Can't figure up goodness. Can't decide
if the real evil is death in the wide ocean,
where the waves could wash you
anywhere, or graves in this thick water,
where nothing ever moves
or gets away.

Library, 1830

That all persons who shall teach, or permit or cause to be taught, any
slave in this State, to read or write, shall, upon conviction thereof,
before any court of competent jurisdiction, be imprisoned, not less
than one month nor more than twelve months. – March 16, 1830,
Louisiana

Grandfather would notice his books
missing, so she held herself until
the world skinned itself in blankets

to light a candle and steal into the dark room
with her own leaky pen and stolen scrap paper
from the post. It had taken four months

of copying pages nightly,
but she had nearly smuggled out every last line
of Grandfather's abridged Odyssey.

You had to do bad sometimes, had to play tricks,
had to sneak to have a good heart,
to guide your good heart home. She climbed

the shelves like a ladder and lifted the spine
she'd have known in the dark,
set up the flickering light on the desk

and flipped to the end. Her fingers,
calloused, half-stained black, shook
as Penelope welcomed her husband home

after so many nights on her own.
She wrote until it was finished,
until the sky in the windows had changed,

then eased the book into its bed,

and ghosted to her room.
In just a few short hours,

when Grandfather and the others were
off on their business, she would sprint the pecan rows
to find Delphine and Miss Jean and Abraham

who would drag their fingers, slick from
cornbread and gristle, along the lines as they read
together. She felt the sting in her eyes and nose.

As the sun rose, she imagined their faces,
saw them cry out after so many months

of watching a man do battle with curses
to find his way home, saw their shoulders
hardened and squared as they stalked

back to the labyrinthine fields
where they would grow old.

Attic, 1835

From the window, he could see
over the long columns of oaks,
south even beyond the packed fields.
The river wound down to the belly
of Terrebonne Bay, a falling off
in the tree line, just visible as the sun
sunk collapsed into the waterline.

His shoulder remembered,
even the next day, the weight
of his father's polished black casket,
the slow music, his mother weeping
in linen. He leaned
against the sill and watched the sun
bake the land and the shoulders
chopping cane to their own music.

In his last minutes, his father had held his face
with the strength of a well man. "This will be
your bed tomorrow. That, your window,
those, your fields. They hunger, boy,
and you will feed them or they'll swallow you."

The fields were his. The shoulders. Even
the music, if he wanted it. So far up, though,
the sound thinned out. His father's voice
rattling from his stone grave above ground
thinned out. He heard only the churning
steady noise of the Mississippi. Like some
great bowel, the river only ever passed
things away. There was no returning,
was never any rising back up
above sea-level.

Barracks, 1839

Abraham shook in the lone wooden chair,
baking in his own sweat. Word was the master,
himself, was coming down this morning
to get an answer for last night's transgressions.

It was just Miss Lively, her wrists and her neck
and her purple Christmas dress, hair unwrapped,
a dried flower or two in it. Damned Miss Lively
and her eyes that Abraham could never catch. What else
could he do? Damned Miss Lively, what else
but steal – borrow, no, borrow – the master's shining
boots, his best horse, and ride down into the barracks
where the music rose up wild and Hello Miss Lively,
care for a dance?

And did she ever. Might as well have sent
those other beggars home. Abraham
could hardly get his breath for turning that woman
in circle after circle, eating up her laughter, her
calling him Mister Abraham Sir cause his boots
mirrored all the firelight.

But then, after he talked her into a kiss,
he went to coax the horse back to his pen,
and that horse had died dead. And wouldn't you know,
not one of those beggars would raise a hand
to help him move the corpse back up the hill.
Damn them all. Jealousy's as vile a sin as stealing.

So he waited, quiet as he could be, the day after
Christmas, and here came the master on his second
best horse, wearing his second best pair of boots.
Grinning. Grinning like he might split in two
with laughing any second. "Abraham, m'boy,
m'boy." He stalked a few slow circles round the room,

all the breath sucked from Abraham's lungs.

"You know we got to go outside, son, and show 'em
what happens to a thief. You know we do."

Abraham couldn't even make words
to say, "I know it, sir."
"But first," the master said, "I ought to say,
we all done wildness for a woman
at least once in our lives. You never
let another man outdo you, son. And keep the boots."

Later, all the flesh gone from his back,
mouth full of blood and a tooth aimed wrong,
Abraham choked down a sob, squeezed shut
his lids, slid into another body, his heart
dancing mad circles. He woke and dropped
back into dreams of those eyes. That flower.

Kitchen, 1845

Violet feels the coming storm in her knees,
less pain than heaviness – the body's way
of speaking with the earth. She grinds
herbs into flakes and dreads
the walks back and forth from the kitchen
to the house – the path slopes up and
makes the ground give way in long rains.

This morning, she stood by as her grown son
fired his knife through the largest pig's
skull. She hurried to slit its throat, to catch
its hot blood in a large tin pail before its heart
stopped beating. Together, they looped a noose
around its neck and dragged it to be butchered
in a clean place.

The first thunder booms. It will not be
long. She uses her hands to mash the herbs
into a bowl of rice, ground pork and blood
still barely warm, to make it rich. She ties off
one end of the pig's rinsed and scraped intestines
stuffs them with her fine red mess,
then twists them off at intervals.

Tonight, she'll smoke boudin noir, set it
on wide wooden trays, cover it with layers of
linen to ward off rain, drag her tired feet
through warm, infested mud, pass her work
to dry house maids, who'll situate the food
on plates, just so. The family will feed
themselves on silver and never think
of Violet, never think to climb down in the dirt,
to plead with her to tell them what secret
pinch of something makes the blood so good.

Back Fields, 1849

Of the one hundred fifty-one fugitive women advertised for
in the 1850 New Orleans newspapers, none was listed as
having run away without her children.

—Deborah Gray White

"After the rains, Del," said Abraham. "After the rains,
we gone." She makes a noise to let him know
she heard. "We gon' leave the lil' thing
with Gray Momma, and we gone. Can't
watch you die, Del. Can't stand the sting."

In the high cane with both of them bent to chop
near the root, they can be alone in their own
way. She moves slow since the baby –
hips never set back right, but he groans
and doubles his stack quick to make up her time.

She makes another noise, feels a swell
of something rotten in her throat. She won't say no,
but knows she can never go. Knows she'll have to see
the back of Abraham, still her boy-faced love.
She won't tell him, though. Won't make him stay.

He holds his big hands out for her stack
and hefts it all back to the wagon. He holds
her hand. She won't tell him till that night,
that night he'll wake her late, all hands and hurry,
all packed already. She'll wait till then.

She'll kiss him, slide the dried flower
she wooed him with into his fist, reach up to kiss
his crooked mouth, give him all the bread
she's laid aside, turn him out into the night
and crawl in beside the little thing, and cry.

Master Bedroom, 1852

She had only just kissed her children
and begun disrobing when
her husband's shoulders filled the door.
A thin sweat sucked the linen
against his flat belly.

August heat revealed everyone, she thought.
Ladies sweated off their fine powder, sticky
rouge. Girls threw their petticoats in piles.
The black bodies slowed their work. Her husband's
blood rose by degrees. He tore at her
underclothes. He had assumed the overseer's
work today in a humid delirium. He had taken
a man's skin off. He was made
of one thousand hands. Some fastened
her necklaces. Held her daughter's
soft skull in the night. He
was powered by steam.

He peeled his breeches off and held her
around the belly like a dead weight.
He broke against her like a storm,
the force of earth beating to destroy
whatever man has built. Beating to destroy
always and remorselessly itself.

Parlor, 1854

The boy couldn't sleep for three nights
after he'd seen his father kill a woman
for the first time.

Men he'd seen hung his whole life,
seen babies born dead. He was a smart boy,
he knew. A brave boy. Always wanted
to see. First out of bed. Couldn't look away.
Afraid to miss anything.

There were boys who looked away, he knew,
like Jackie Hebert who hid in his toybox
when the maid went out to kill chickens,
who faked fever to avoid the autumn hunt.
He'd even begged off cleaning his own fish
last summer in the bay.

There was wrong in that, his father'd said.
His father'd said a boy shouldn't eat anything
he couldn't kill and clean himself.

But that night, after he saw the woman, the boy
walked the parlor after he'd soaked his sheets,
after his room'd shrunk so small he couldn't
get his breath good. Naked. Like the woman
had been naked. There was wrong in that.

Thing was, part of the boy felt warm sometimes,
something good like love for Jackie Hebert
and his gentle heart that needed guarding,
and the boy cleaned Jackie's fish for him that summer
and was happy to do it. One boy could catch enough fish
for four boys. No reason to dirty everyone's hands.

It took work to wring the fish smell out of skin.

The boy rested his head against the cool piano,
tried to fill his mouth with saliva. Froth had pooled
around her lips. He wondered what that felt like,
wondered what she'd done

that made his father rise up before dawn,
wake the property in the gray light
to lash her even after all her life had run out.

He had never seen breasts before that morning.
He couldn't wring them out of his head
which he eased down onto the cold keys
until they uttered a low groan.
His father was a good man, he thought,
as he wrapped his arms around himself,
pressed his short nails into his own shoulders,
just to see how it felt. Harder. How it felt.

When the keys went slick under his head,
he knew he was crying. He nestled his nose
between the black keys and let it happen.

You couldn't look away. Jackie Hebert
was a coward who hid with his toys. He chewed
on his tongue and his lips. A boy couldn't eat
what he wouldn't kill. The boy let the spittle

drip out of his mouth. His head slid down,
his nose wedged between the black keys.
His rest-starved heart did not speed
as his mind clipped from breasts to beasts
to chickens and toys and dark boxes
to blood to fever to froth and at last to a long,
long life of the ungodliest hunger.

Grand Ballroom, 1859

Pearl spat with force on the master's floor
and wiped in circles with her whole body. The word
was war and her sons were in fits. They'd weather
whole nights up with Old Israel studying stars
like a map to another world.

The world was too wide to think on. The chandelier
threw stars of its own in the waxed wood and Pearl
pictured all the pairs of feet who would be circling
it soon, constellations crushed under fine white slippers
to polished violins. There would be no place
on the land to unhear the music, to escape its cadence

and they would fall asleep with a waltz in their ears.
How long would it hang there? she wondered.
Would it have their feet falling in three-four time
in the grand high cane in the sun? Would it spin
them in circles even after this summer? After
a war? After ten thousand star-guided steps?

Back Porch, 1862

"You here, Missus? I cain't see not a thing."

The woman tugged her soft robe around herself
and watched Liza limp up to the porch in the darkness.
"I'm here, Liza," she said, holding out her pale hand.

"You boil that water and get you a cup like I asked?"
The woman, who shook even in the summer evening,
nearly said "Yes ma'am," but caught herself.

Old Liza, clacking her lantern down on the wood,
reminded the woman of a crumbling, ancient goddess,
a dusty sibyl with a spell for everything.

But she knew this was not magic, knew all the magic
had dried up from the earth like the streams
in drought. This was the dust left behind.

"Missus, you know now, you know your husband
cain't know about this. You tell him – I'll get strung up
like a windchime. Give me that hot water, now, and your word."

The woman handed Liza the cup of scalding water,
said her promises, pressed her forearms
into her own stomach. Inside, her husband

lay sprawled in the bed, exhausted, no doubt,
from his nightly war on her body. Liza produced
purple flowers ("Pennyroyal, Missus") from her pocket,

shredded the leaves, dropped them in the water to steep.
The woman lifted the cup to her mouth, but Liza,
brown skin shining in the lantern light, grabbed her arm.

"You drink that, ain't no coming back from it. Thing'll be gone

like it never was." The woman's stomach turned,
but she parted her lips and swallowed the tea all at once.

Liza pressed her own lips together and nodded her head.
"I think you a good woman, Missus," she said.
The woman thought the tea might come back up.

"Go on back to your bed, Liza," the woman whispered,
wiping her mouth with her sleeve like a savage.
"He'll never know. You always tell me what you need,

and you'll have it." Liza patted her arm, scooped up
her lantern, and made her way off. The light grew smaller
through the minutes, like a soul with no body

steering the long dry road out of the world.

Sugar House, 1864

Old Israel sat alone in the dark with dead cane,
tying and untying rope. The rot had taken his feet,
the overseer his wife, the Union his sons.

The fields were empty now – the others fled
to chase freedom, a piece of meat
hung before a dog.

He'd sent them, flung them, towards it, fought them
when they tried to carry him. A man grows heavy
with years, too heavy to be lifted, too old

to be moved. He spat and slapped when they tried
to say prayers on him. How fast they forgot
the old gods. How quick they were to love the almighty.

There were so many men, and just one lonesome god.
If life was a numbers game, the Lord would be dead,
strung up by his bent-backed flock for his wrongs.

God was a weed you couldn't kill. A brutal fisherman
with hooks, and all the fish in the world couldn't get to him.
To do battle, you got to be able to breathe.

Breath lost its luster after too long. Old sugar stank.
A breeze had the nerve to blow as he slung
the rope over the mightiest beam.

The Inner Stair, 1887

The untreated cypress sunk in the centers
of each step, bent by ten thousand errands
done in darkness. Quite alone inside
the unlit spiral, it seemed the violins,
the clanking cups, the broken French
drifted in from another house.

She had never used these stairs,
and no one would look for her here.

There were no candles permitted
in the inner stair – the fear of fire
ruled the corridor. In the dark, champagne-
dulled, she tried to feel time.

Was it possible? Had it only been hours?
The girl felt lifetimes had passed through her
bones since they had blessed the food,
since her silk-suited cousins, strangers
with fine hair, had come off the boat
to see the property and inquire
whether they might buy stock. She felt
years had blown by since the polished city
families had strolled the front lawns
before turning each other in careful dances
on the freshly-waxed floors.

So wide were her skirts,
no maid, not even with a warrant
for clean cups or fresh candles, not even
with her father's orders, could pass her.
Her own breaths rebounded in the closeness.

Sometimes even in the blackness,
eyes made useless, you could feel how small

the world was around you.
There were fools who would believe
the red-faced pair of dinner guests
only took the serving maid
behind the house, her elbows in their hands,
to ask her questions or redress some wrongdoing.

There were wise men, fine party hosts,
who called for another dance to cover the noise,
who perspired and called it too much wine,
who would sort the matter out in the gravity
of tomorrow's daylight.

And there were women in between, women
who bent stairs or hid on them, girls without
candles who saw everything in the darkness.

Nursery, 1892

> The son can do nothing of himself, but what he seeth the
> father do: for what things soever he doeth, these also doeth
> the son likewise.
>
> —John 5:19

He'd have preferred a daughter. His sleeping son's
fingers gripped his shirt sleeves. He shifted
in his chair so his whiskers would not rough
the boy's pink cheek. He had been a baby, himself,

in this room – had bobbled on his small boy legs,
had stacked blocks in towers, jingled bells
to coax out the ring of his mother's laughter.
And then, he had grown into his feet,
out of the nursery, into the darker rooms:
ledgers by lamplight, windows
overlooking the high cane. He had not missed
his hands' slow hardening. He had not missed
the way his heart hurt less each summer.

The sun would soon rise in the window.
His son would freckle in its light some day
as he walked the rows to observe
spring growth, as he held the soil in his fist
to sense its readiness. The boy's hands, tugging
on his collar, could not fathom their fate.

As the dawn threatened, he feared the boy,
feared already that his son reflected him
like windowglass in the evening.
What could a father want for his boy more than this?
What broken soul held his son only in the darkness?

A daughter he could have covered
with a fine wide hat, buttoned gloves. To her,

he would not have to say, "Go and figure up
how much the earth owes you, what you'll do
to pull out one more season's fruit."

A daughter he could have guarded,
could have stroked and sung to, could have
reminded that the earth was gentle
and built to bloom her flowers,
and by the light of day,
he could have made her believe it.

Front Porch, 1900

They sequestered the children and the old
woman whose mind had begun to go
to the front porch in the afternoons. It was built
to catch breezes and to keep the troubled
and the troubling out from under the feet
of the busy women. Reports from town
measured one hundred fourteen degrees. Her withering
white hair clung to her freckled neck.
Everything was dead, brown from the house
to the skinny green line of the river.

"Another Rastus story, Granny," the little boy
begged as the smaller girl crawled on her stiff knees.

"I don't know as I have another in me,"
she said, goading. She'd been growing the stories
her maid had told her as a child of the man Rastus
on his riverboat with his lucky rabbit's foot.

"But Granny! Does he get away
from the robbers? Granny please!"

She'd started to pick up the tale where
she'd left it, but as the waving rhythm
of the rocker found pace with her breathing,
the names and places left her mind.
She stroked the little girl's long braid,
but could not call up her name.

"She's havin' a spell," the boy whispered
to his sister. "Let's go hide
in the cane. She'll never find us."

"You mustn't!" the old woman croaked
and lit to her feet, the little girl hitting

the wood with a thud. "You mustn't dally
in the back fields. Nothing but death
for a thousand acres!" She nearly fell
back into her chair.
resumed rocking. "And who knows,"
she whispered, looking at no one.
"Who knows what demons
may lurk in the earth?"

Milk House, 1905

On Sundays after church he liked to wander
down to the milk house and watch the girl
Roberta skim the cream off the vat's surface
and work it madly in the churn.

He was tall by then and understood himself
but didn't figure he had mastered anything
like she had done that milk. He'd sneak
bread from the kitchen and tear

it to share with her. They buttered it with
their fingers. Hers were rough and dry
the one time he'd brushed them, and he
tried to hide his smooth unblemished palms.

She said his first name like a secret, slow,
not like his mother said it. He brought her
presents she refused. He brushed a moth
out of her hair, which felt like warm wool.

Later, his hands still slick and cheeks on fire,
he wondered if she had any soft places,
or if her whole body was secrets and hard-
spun and how hot you'd have to get her
to make her melt.

Widow's Walk, 1918

The word came that seven hundred thousand
bodies had drawn their last breaths at Verdun,
an earth-quaking number for those unacquainted
with the greedy appetites of death.
She had never been across the sea, but pictured
the corpses laid in neat rows like chopped cane
at harvest time.

"Apologies, ma'am," came Small John's voice
from the rear stairs. "I'd'a sent Roberta,
but she scared fiercely of high places.
You got to come down. The sun will cook
you through."

Five weeks her husband had been gone,
and she hadn't even heaved a sigh until
she'd tried to fasten her silver bracelet on her own,
a task best suited to a second pair of hands.
Sweating, she gripped the chain until the metal
grew hot in her palm.

"Ma'am?" Small John tried again. Without
turning, she could feel him moving closer.
Had he ever touched her once in these long years?
"Roberta said you in a fury."

She turned from the iron railing and flung
the bracelet at him hard. It hit his shoulder,
tinkled as it fell onto the slate.
He lifted it by one end like a snake
and walked toward her. "I'd'a gone, too,"
he said. "Over there to fight. 'Cept I don't
see like I ought to, and my knee ain't right."

He watched her as if she might bolt

over the edge, her body set to lunge. Her
temper cooled quick, the way summer
afternoons went from sweltering to raising
shivers on skin before a hurricane
blew in from the gulf. "Small John?" she asked.
She held her shaking wrist out to him, her jaw
and throat and chest all gone hot and raw.

She thought he might throw it back at her,
but he looked at her straight on, barely glanced
down as he slipped the tiny teeth
of the clasp together around her wrist, never
once touched her skin.

Library, 1922

Since the father had dragged home from war,
he took his meals alone. He kissed no one
and did not answer questions,
but spoke daily to God in whispers.

The boy slept in his father's reading chair
until the softness had abandoned it, and slept there
still, the chair holding him and smelling like his father
had when he still polished it and smoked.
And when he woke, as he often did, deep in the night,
he skipped his little fingers over the old bindings
and felt choked by all there was to know.

The father stocked the lower shelves,
the ones the son could reach, with books
he said were safe. The too-high volumes
the boy would have to wonder over
until he grew tall.

The Bible's spine was bent to Job,
which the boy could not keep himself from
turning to, a book the boy reckoned his father
ought to have shelved higher up.

Often he returned to those pages of death
at God's hands and shuddered. He pictured
seven thousand sheep on fire, a cotton field
eaten up with worms, hot black boils, the way
a mighty wind, just like a hurricane, could fell
a house and kill him, kill his sisters
in one big breath.

When the father thought he was alone,
he asked the lord for absolution, prayed often
for deliverance from a sin he would not name.

Perhaps the boy would understand
when he could touch any book he liked.

He would not ask, though. No matter
how tall he ever grew, how many years went by.
He'd never ask his father how much a man had to lose
before he could prove his goodness
in the far-off eye of God.

Child's Bedroom, 1933

She sat in a hard rocker by the boy's poster bed
when everyone had gone to sleep. His mother
wouldn't hear any backtalk about it – no matter
that Berta had been up three nights straight with him,
that she'd pulled up every weed in Terrebonne Parish
this morning on bad knees in the bald sun.

He'd snap himself in half with coughing, and she
would draw the heavy water basin close, ring out
a strip cut from flour sacks and dab at him, fan him
to put off the dampness. Oil and sweat
layered his purpling eyelids, his soapy sinking
cheeks. His young man's temper, bright and hot
in him, was flattened out by fever. His toys,
passed down and overused, needed dusting now.

He'd spat on her once when nobody else could see.
He couldn't say but a few words back then,
he was so small. But he could spit hard like a man.
And if he hadn't broken more dishes
than she could recall – took joy in it, too.
He'd slide them, plates and saucers, to the edge
of the supper table, scoot them with his little finger,
a breath at a time, like a contest against himself.
When they came undone with a cry on the wood
floors, he smiled in private triumph.

She was half asleep in her chair when he shrieked
"Berta!" through cracked lips, the first sound
he'd made in days. She should wake his mother,
let her see her oldest boy's eyes open, but she couldn't
quite make herself rise up. The boy reached
for the water near his bed, splashed it with his fist onto
the rug. Beat hard on Berta's arm when she tried
to sponge his mouth with her linen rag.

And then, his eyes turned back into his head
like Berta'd seen in others with the yellow sickness
just before life left them flat.
She couldn't ever say why she just sat,
never rang or cried out for another soul. Just rocked,
her soil-roughed hands folded on her knees.
His body twitched a while, bowels loosed,
breath slowed and raced and slowed. Death's unfed
fingers had him, but toyed with him a while, drew him
up to the very precipice of gray eternity by increments
of eyelashes until there was nothing left
but to watch him tumble over and rejoice.

Dining Room, 1943

Berta and Eloise bring in the ham
on the good crystal, wish everyone
a happy Easter, which everyone returns.

The father prays, gives thanks for the son
who remains, squeezes his wife's hand.
The dead child's place is pregnant with him
even after nine rounds of spring. The son
who's left serves his parents' plates.

"Have you enjoyed your break from school?"
his mother asks. Then, "Son? You're pale.
Is it too warm?"

The son stares long at his dead brother's chair.
"I won't return to school. I'm joining up
with Will Favreux first thing tomorrow."

When they hear glass shatter,
Berta and Eloise dash in with fingers still
sticky from their share of ham.
"What in the name of heaven," Eloise says,
eyes wide at the pile of shattered crystal,
the floor slick with tea.

"Now we got to talk about this," says his father,
bending with Eloise to gather the large chunks of glass,
eyes on his wife as he speaks to his son.
"You're all set for Loyola in the fall. There's scores
of young men to go fight."

Berta stays straight-backed and makes no move
to attend to the mess. "I'll not be conscripted,"
the son says. "I'll not have my name called
like a doomed man. I won't let them say that

I hid in this house."

His mother looks like she might throw more glass,
and his father holds her shoulders leaving Eloise
to the floor. The son excuses himself
unable to sit a moment longer across from
his dead brother, his mother gone cold.

Berta follows him into the kitchen,
stands next to him as he stares out the garden window.
He leans against her and she lets him.
"Quentin goin', too," she whispers.
"You watch out for my boy."

He doesn't know it, but in a few weeks,
he'll be sleeping in French mud and red water.
He'll make a sad pile of rags
into a pillow, and the last thing he'll think of
before the starlight leaves his eyes
will be the smell of honey on Berta's fingers
as she held him like a small boy
in his mother's house.

Lavatory, 1949

He figures his mother intends to skin him
alive with her bristly sponge. If he leaks
any sound, she'll come at him again with
"If you'd only do what you're told..."

The waiting room at Dr. LaFitte's office
had been so dull — just baby toys and nothing
to drink but fountain water. And when
he'd heard the children's voices from behind
a door he'd never seen opened, he had to see.

She takes to his back until it feels like
every sunburn and wasp sting and flake
of red pepper he's ever had all at once.
The bathwater has gone cold and cloudy.

He'd waited until his mother excused
herself to powder her sweating nose and hightailed
to that door. It was stiff on its hinges and scraped
when he shoved it open. The children
on the other side froze when they saw him.

"If I told your father, you'd be tanned clean,"
she said. She hadn't, though. She unstopped
the drain and jerked him up by his armpits.
The boy had never before looked at his mother
and seen a girl, quite unsure.

Those other children were bored, too, waiting on
the doctor. No toys at all in their room. No floor,
either, which suited them fine as the boy joined
them building trenches in the red dirt.

Back Porch, 1952

The air was so packed with heat, the girl
felt herself frying, wondered how hot
you'd have to be before you'd start to crisp
like chicken with the skin still on.

To think about what she'd done, her mother said.
"Sit in the heat a while. Think about the kind
of girl we raised you to be. Think about that, now."
All she could think about was the four layers
of clothes she was wearing, thick and pasted together
against her legs.

She'd been planning to ask the question
for weeks, had a time and place all set – when
her mother and father were drowsing, perhaps,
or deep in their cups. But questions have a way
of driving themselves up in their own time,
like blades of grass shooting through the slats
of the old porch, or hairs sprouting
where they're not wanted.

"Is Berta a nigger?"

Her mother had slapped her face
for the first time. The noise surprised her
more than the sting. Her father said nothing.
Berta, who she thought had gone home,
cleared her throat from the next room, walked in,
and asked if anyone needed anything else.

The deep grey paint on the wood held heat
and bit into her palms when she tried to lean back
on them. Think about what you've done. She
would not ask a question again as long as she could
stand it. She was so thirsty. Sit in the heat

a while. She felt her mother's hand scorched above her jaw. Think about the kind of girl we raised you to be.

Master Bedroom, 1960

The water's porch-high
and it's three weeks too early when his wife
loses her water on the commode.

Collette has lit lamps, has informed him
the phones are down, has brought him
a triple tumbler of scotch, half of which
he's hurled at her for troubling him while his wife
screams the paint off the walls. She dabs at the whiskey

and whispers, "Mistuh Claude, my granny
Berta, she taught me how to bring a child.
I count seven I brought into the world, now."

His ulcer, which he's only ever felt at the office,
spews acid into his stomach. "She needs a doctor,"
he says to the painting in the hall. "She needs
the twilight sleep. Not some jungle ritual. Not
some back alley medicine woman."

Glass shatters in the bedroom. Thunder
ushers in new waves of storm. "Ain't no doctor
gone' swim to your house, sir. It's the back alley
or a dead wife hardly twenty years old.
Let me get in there, now."

He isn't sure if his body consents, but in
she goes, him after her, hiding his body
behind her body, anything to keep from seeing
his wife's body which can only make noises, which can
only breathe in great loud pulls.

His girl, who he kissed under the front oaks,
welcomes Collette's dry hands under her belly,
allows her knees to be eased open, even smiles

in an exhausted way, as the maid examines
her insides.

"You been pushin?" Collete asks
in a voice he has never heard before,
the way he would talk to his baby, if his baby came.
His wife says she can't push anymore, she's through,
there's nothing left. Collette leans back,
wipes her hand on her apron, and says,
"Get on your knees, Ma'am."

All in one breath, all like a crash, he's got Collette
by the hair, got her neck jerked back like a snake.
"Over my dead body," he seethes, letting his "B"
throw spit on her face.

"Yo child's shoulder lodged up behind her bones,"
she said, not fighting his grip. "It ain't gone' come
on its own. This'll set her hips wide, and I'ma
get it out for ya. But you got to let me go."

Before he loosens his hold, his wife has already
rolled herself over, seething and bleeding and soaking
and holding herself on her hands and knees.
"Do it," she says in a language of groans. "You let her go
Claude. I'm half-dead."

As far as he remembers, that child
was conceived in the dark: his wife
in a nightgown, both of them under thin sheets
with their eyes clamped shut and their faces
turned in opposite directions.

But there she is now, his bride – naked at the waist,
red, wailing on all fours like an animal in the dirt,
the negro maid's arm jammed past the wrist
inside her, maid's shoulders squared like a soldier,

her voice so soft he can hardly hear it.

The storm shutters knock around hard,
and he'll always remember his son coming
into a world with a mother bent over, a maid
cooing orders, covered in whiskey
and blood, rain rising into the house,
and a father who understood none of it.

Kitchen, 1964

For five dollars extra, Collette coats
and boots her girl before dawn on Christmas
morning and they slip into the Belle Mar
with an old brass key and work at a feast,
quietly, per instruction, so as not to wake
the children. But baking bread has a way

of coaxing boys from their beds, and little
boy feet pad close and tug at her
fingers. How can she not house some love
for a boy who would bypass a tree strewn
with gifts to come have a bite of fresh bread.

And of course, the girl is of no use
with the boy awake. She makes them a game
of pressing cloves into oranges and gives
them both a little milk with coffee in it.
Quietly, they sit until the sun works in
through the windows, and then, they hardly breathe.

Knowing the house will not wake
for an hour or two, she lets them slip on
the grown people's shoes and walk out,
one fastened to each of her knees. Never
having seen snow before, they are afraid
it might hurt, but cannot stop laughing
when at last they bury their bare hands
in the perfect and untouched glorious cold.

Grand Staircase, 1970

The boy, who should have been asleep,
lowered himself in the elbow of the staircase
where he wouldn't be seen. Collette had tucked
him in early to ready the house for the party.

Through the yellow glass windows, he saw
the women around citronella candles
on the front porch smoking cigarettes,
while their husbands uncapped beers
on the striped sofas and made bets
on Ali and Bonavena.

The boy didn't understand boxing – at least
not beyond the young doomed hero's punches
he'd thrown in the yard at St. Mark's.
But the dancing man, the one who floated,
who talked like music, who boasted
like a giant unafraid to die, that he stayed awake for.

"Jimmy, you in the pool? What you reckon?"
asked his father. "Hundred says that fuckin'
draft dodger's gonna be on his black ass
by the end of the night," Jimmy called back to laughs
and jeers and a din of men taking his odds.
The boy thought for a moment that he ought to heave
his coffee can of nickels, so heavy
it took two hands to lift, down there
and see if that wouldn't hush Jimmy LaFleur right up.

He'd dreamt the night before that he was in
Madison Square Garden – it looked like a garden
in his dream – and Ali came and showed him
how to shut a man down. In his dream,
Ali came home and showed those boys at St. Mark's
who owned what.

41

The first bell rang, and the boy forced his face
between the rails of the staircase. The men were sweating
and red-cheeked as they hollered out. His father
was an Ali man as well, and after fourteen rounds,
was saying a rosary for him loud enough
for everyone to hear.

Three hard socks to Bonavena in the fifteenth
and he was down, and the boy thought to hell
with bed times, and he fired out his victorious roar
with the other men. His father, covered in sweat,
heard him over the crowd, and ran to the boy,
hoisted him into the air.

The boy closed his eyes, imagined
Ali's heartbeat pounding in his chest,
imagined he, himself, had danced
under those lights.

Tool Shed, 1980

he makes a pillow of the sheet
his mother kneels on to garden and
lays the girl's head on it

when he angles her hips up to receive him,
she cocks her chin backwards
and he can see down her throat for centuries

and back to that moment he saw her
skin the color of barely-creamed coffee, eyes
green like peppermint, black pepper freckles

walking the Quarter selling maps to tourists
and then her eyes open wide and she
tightens around him and he kisses her

so the sound won't carry to the house
and she's never asked why they couple
beside the edger and sheers and wound up hoses

each time he brings her here,
the world doubles in size, fills up
with more things he'll never really know...

what she's really saying when he makes her
come on the floor and she cries out in four
languages at once

what she'd look like in his bed
sheets bunched up in her toes
lousy with jewels

Attic, 1988

"Would it be alright," Collette had asked,
"for me to bring my lil grandson to play
over here? I see your girl got them chicken pox –
they say it's better to get that ugliness overwith
while you're young. Hurts bad when you grown."

The man, who bore a few pockmarks himself
from a late bout, heartily agreed. The children
sat on their diapered bottoms in the cool attic
hollering into a red plastic karaoke machine
and examining themselves in his grandmother's
antique stand mirror.

Collette returned to her ironing and left the man
to attend them a while. When they bored of music,
and their reflections, he made a game of bouncing them
one on each knee, and making horse noises.
Even with their boiling laughter in his ears,

he didn't miss how strange it was to will a child sick.
But it all made sick sense. Too bad, he thought,
holding them around their plump bellies,
we couldn't get all the sickness out
of the way while we were small, before
we'd remember the hurt.

Too bad, he said to himself, (the children
turned wild, climbing him with abandon)
we couldn't exit the loud tangle of childhood
immune to life's long afflictions. Unable
to keep still, the little monsters toddled
to the picture window facing the back fields
and pressed their lips
and sticky fingers against the glass,

thrilled by how high up they were. It was only three stories,
but when the man leaned over and pressed
his own nose against the cool pane
and looked straight down, the overgrown land
seemed, indeed, so far below them,
it would take a lifetime of falling to reach it.

Sugar House, 1992

"Collette," she'd asked their graying maid,
"why's there paintings on the walls
in the sugar house? You can't see them
no more hardly. How come they didn't
use paper?" Collette poured iced tea
into a purple plastic cup and served
Emmaline sandwiches jelly-side up, cut diagonally.
"I guess we use what we got, miss Emmaline.
Like you got to wipe yo nose sometimes an' I
catch you with yo sleeve all sloppy."

She should have been asleep this afternoon,
but sneaked down the back stairs with fistfuls
of old school papers, spread them out face down
in a wide circle on the ragged wood floor, kicked
dried sticks of cane out of her way. The faded
women on the walls washed their clothes
in the bayou nearby.

Her daddy once turned her backside
red when she spoke back to him, and said
that her little behind would remember it
any time she dared to speak like that again.

It did remember. And if it could, what else
had memories? Her pillow with the purple
sham remembered her head heavy
with sleep, folded down just right in welcome.
She drew it, ridged with the pattern
of floor. Drew her bed. The floor showed
through it, too. Did floors remember, then,
the whooping they had taken – feel fear
when the storms came in summer to make them
swell with water? If floors did,
could the whole house

remember, too?

Child's Bathroom, 2000

"Be still now, or you'll spend your first day
of high school lopsided." The girl forced a smile
at the joke and sat as still as she could,
but sadness – beyond just summer's end –
breathed with a slow rain through the open curtains.

"If you cut it all off, my momma'd be so embarrassed
maybe I could stay home." There was nothing
for hair like this, truth be told. No potion
to make it lay right. No outgrowing it, either.

"And I'd be fired. Hold still now." Collette trimmed
the bangs into a rough line, blew the leftovers
softly off the girl's freckled nose. "School ain't s'bad,
missy. You're almost a lady. Ain't you pleased?"

The girl rubbed her lips together, staring
at their reflection, swallowed by her overgrown hair.
Collette knew they were cruel to her at school,
heard they'd laughed when her blood came
down her knee in gym, knew they'd ignored
her party invitations.

"Sometimes," Collete said, "trimming ends
helps hair grow." The scissors clicked across
the hem of the girl's hair. "People grow older –
those bad parts get cut. It gets smoother
as you go along."

Oh, but Collette's girl was wise, she was.
Could sense lies like old knees
foretold ugly weather.
Collette gave up the scissors
and combed the girl's hair with her fingers,
the way she used to soothe her before the world went bad.

"Quit that cryin', baby. You know I'm making
your favorite thing for supper. You walk straight
in the mornin'. You walk straight all the days
comin'. It gets easier as they grow. They got to catch
up with you, is all."

Collette just wanted to hold her sweet girl,
but she couldn't. The untruth was a gulf
between them. No one outgrew much. Seasons passed
and hair turned gray. But hearts that started bad
only changed as much as water turning into ice -
a shift in state, a hardening, no way to trim it down.

Old hates collected, smoothed out by time,
froze and expanded, set and safe enough
to walk across without losing your step,
but too hard to crack open for a drink,
and sometimes you just had to thirst all your life.

The Belle Mar, 2005

Jefferson Parish reports:
of all the babies born there
at the end of August, not one was named
Katrina.

The grown girl brought her gray parents iced tea
on the damp porch. They hadn't wanted
to go inside and see.
They sat on the steps,
the rocking chairs in pieces far away.
There had only been plastic cups left
in the kitchen cabinets.
Her mother drank from hers
and didn't ask.

Her father put his bent hand
on his wife's knee. "We'll build it back
like it was," he promised.

"Oh, what for?" her mother groaned,
her eyes glossing as they scanned
the rows of ruined oaks.

A breeze blew from the south,
carried the watery air through the blown-out
windows, brought the smell
of rot, a great stink from the mouth
of the land.

If her old maid Collette had been alive,
she would have marched right into the mess
with a broom and a bucket of rags.

Everything good was dead.

She'd grown up in the house's haunted halls,
memorized the abstract faces in the wood grains,
asked questions about the back buildings
which never did receive answers.
The back buildings were gone now,
probably floating somewhere in the Gulf.
She wasn't a girl anymore, and didn't have
any questions.

Her father patted her mother's knee.
She couldn't stand to see
the once-majestic pair
holding each other's old bodies
in front of the filthy white columns.
She made off to examine the fields,
and heard her father say, "Just like it was.
I promise."

She believed him. He would sink his last dime
into raising the house from this ruin.
But in her marrow, hope rose
like floodwater, hope
the house was finished,
swallowed finally by the earth
that had never wanted it,
the way skin grows up over a burn,
the way blood in a river
washes out and disappears
in the open arms of the waiting, beautiful sea.

Parlor, 2012

My mother died and left a key that unlocked
every room and a slip of paper with instructions
for the rest of my life.

Sit with your knees together.
Don't let a man see you sweat or weep.
Red shoes are for hookers and elves.
Recipes are secondary to your heart.
Remember the foundations you are built on.
Guard against the rattling bayou ghosts,
the pinstuck bones who stalk the riverline.
There are bayou ghosts down
Carry a talisman always.

My mother was mistaken. Ghosts stay
close to home, grinding their teeth
in the walls, making their beds
in the warped floors. I see them
sweeping out of rooms just as I light lamps.
This is no place to live alone.

Tell me, Mother, how to remember you,
what name to call you and what to absolve.
Tell me how to live on this land. How
many times must I scour and sun the long line
of our lives until the water runs clean.

Tell me yes. Say you want me to rise up
from this floor and
unlock each heavy door at last.
Let me live here. Let me love you
even after I have seen
inside the darkest passages.

About the Author

Katie Bickham earned her MFA from Stonecoast at the University of Southern Maine and currently teaches creative writing at Bossier Parish Community College in Louisiana. In addition to winning the Lena-Miles Wever Todd Poetry Prize from Pleiades Press and the Jeffrey E. Smith Editor's Prize from *The Missouri Review*, her work has appeared in *Pleiades*, *The Missouri Review*, *Prairie Schooner*, *Deep South Magazine*, and elsewhere. Katie lives in Shreveport, Louisiana with her husband and son in a very old house.

Acknowledgements

My gratitude to Jaime Baker for her guidance in the matters of early midwifery, the Terrebonne Parish Historical and Cultural Society for being such gracious teachers, and to all of the citizens below sea level who let me eat their food, walk their homes, and listen to their stories.

Thanks to the journals where versions of the following poems were first published:

Dining Room, 1811 *The Missouri Review*
Kitchen, 1845 *The Missouri Review*
Back Fields, 1849 *Prairie Schooner*
Master Bedroom, 1852 *The Missouri Review*
Back Porch, 1862 *Pleiades*
Front Porch, 1900 *The Missouri Review*
Widow's Walk, 1918 *The Missouri Review*
Child's Bedroom, 1933 *The Missouri Review*
Parlor, 2012 *The Missouri Review*

About the Series

The editors and directors of the Lena-Miles Wever Todd Poetry Series select 10-15 finalists from among those submitted each year. A judge of national renown then chooses one winner for publication. All selections are made blind to authorship in an open competition for which any poet writing in English is eligible. Lena-Miles Wever Todd Prize-winning books are distributed by Louisiana State University Press.

Previous Winners

Sylph, by Abigail Cloud
(selected by Dana Levin)

The Glacier's Wake, by Katy Didden
(selected by Melissa Kwasny)

Paradise, Indiana by Bruce Snider
(selected by Alice Friman)

What's this, Bombadier? by Ryan Flaherty
(selected by Alan Michael Parker)

Self-Portrait with Expletives by Kevin Clark
(selected by Martha Collins)

Pacific Shooter by Susan Parr
(selected by Susan Mitchell)

It was a terrible cloud at twilight by Alessandra Lynch
(selected by James Richardson)

Compulsions of Silkworms & Bees by Julianna Baggott
(selected by Linda Bierds)

Snow House by Brian Swann
(selected by John Koethe)

Motherhouse by Kathleen Jesme
(selected by Thylias Moss)

Lure by Nil Michals
(selected by Judy Jordan)

The Green Girls by John Blair
(selected by Cornelius Eady)

A Sacrificial Zinc by Matthew Cooperman
(selected by Susan Ludvigson)

The Light in Our House by Al Maginnes
(selected by Betty Adcock)

Strange Wood by Kevin Prufer
(selected by Andrea Hollander Budy)

PLEIADES
P R E S S